RUBÁIYÁT OF OMAR KHAYYÁM

The First Version of

EDWARD FITZGERALD

LONDON

THE FOLIO SOCIETY

1955

The Folio Society acknowledges its indebted-
ness to Professor S. Najib Ashraf Nadvi for
kind permission to reproduce the miniatures
included in this edition

SECOND IMPRESSION 1959

SET IN JOANNA TYPE AND
PRINTED IN GREAT BRITAIN
AT THE UNIVERSITY PRESS, OXFORD

*

BOUND BY WEBB SON & CO. LTD.
IN BROCADE SPECIALLY SUPPLIED BY
BRITISH CELANESE LTD

FOREWORD

OMAR KHAYYAM was born at Naishapur in Khorassan about the middle of the eleventh century. During a long life of study he became renowned and respected for his knowledge and wisdom, especially in astronomy and philosophy, and was one of the eight men appointed by Malik Shah to reform the calendar. He wrote many poems in Arabic and Persian, but they contained a freedom of thought distasteful to orthodox Mohammedans, and it was on his scientific and philosophical studies that his fame among his countrymen rested.

The collection of quatrains known as the Rubaiyat was discovered in a Persian manuscript in the Bodleian, and a transcript was sent to the poet FitzGerald by his friend Professor Cowell. FitzGerald's masterly free translation of the verses was published by Quaritch in

1859 and was a complete failure. A copy was bought from the publisher's penny box by Rossetti, who introduced it to Swinburne and Meredith; and it was owing to the influence of these powerful critics that the Rubaiyat achieved universal fame.

This edition is illustrated with miniatures from a recently discovered manuscript dated 911 AH, believed to be the earliest, and probably the only Persian illuminated manuscript of the poem. The costly pigments used suggest that it was prepared for some royal personage, such as the Sultan Husayn Bayqara, one of the foremost patrons of art in the East. For him in Herat worked the great painter and miniaturist Bihzad, and it is probable that the miniature facing the opening stanzas was executed by him. The other miniatures, though perhaps lacking the master touch of Bihzad himself, are undoubtedly of the same school.

AWAKE! for Morning in the Bowl of Night
Has flung the Stone* that puts the Stars to Flight:
    And Lo! the Hunter of the East has caught
The Sultan's Turret in a Noose of Light.

2   Dreaming when Dawn's Left Hand* was in the Sky,
    I heard a Voice within the Tavern cry,
        'Awake, my Little ones, and fill the Cup,
    Before Life's Liquor in its Cup be dry.'

3   And as the Cock crew, those who stood before
    The Tavern shouted — 'Open then the Door!
        You know how little while we have to stay,
    And, once departed, may return no more.'

4   Now the New Year reviving old Desires,
      The thoughtful Soul to Solitude retires,
          Where the WHITE HAND OF MOSES* on the Bough
      Puts out, and Jesus from the Ground suspires.

5   Irám* indeed is gone with all its Rose,
      And Jamshýd's Sev'n-ring'd Cup* where no one knows;
          But still the Vine her ancient Ruby yields,
      And still a Garden by the Water blows.

6   And David's Lips are lock't; but in divine
      High-piping Péhlevi,* with 'Wine! Wine! Wine!
          Red Wine!' — the Nightingale cries to the Rose,
      That yellow Cheek of hers t' incarnadine.

7   Come, fill the Cup, and in the Fire of Spring
      The Winter Garment of Repentance fling:
          The Bird of Time has but a little way
      To fly — and Lo! the Bird is on the Wing

8 And look — a thousand Blossoms with the Day
Woke — and a thousand scatter'd into Clay:
    And this first Summer Month that brings the Rose
Shall take Jamshýd and Kaikobád away.

9 But come with old Khayyám and leave the Lot
Of Kaikobád and Kaikhosrú* forgot:
    Let Rustum* lay about him as he will,
Or Hátim Tai* cry Supper — heed them not.

10 With me along some strip of Herbage strown
That just divides the desert from the sown,
    Where name of Slave and Sultán scarce is known,
And pity Sultán Máhmúd on his Throne.

11 Here with a Loaf of Bread beneath the Bough,
A Flask of Wine, a Book of Verse — and Thou
    Beside me singing in the Wilderness —
And Wilderness is Paradise enow.

12   'How sweet is mortal Sovranty!' — think some:
      Others — 'How blest the Paradise to come!'
        Ah, take the Cash in hand and waive the Rest;
      Oh, the brave Music of a distant Drum!*

13   Look to the Rose that blows about us — 'Lo,
      Laughing,' she says, 'into the World I blow:
        At once the silken Tassel of my Purse
      Tear, and its Treasure on the Garden throw.'

14   The Worldly Hope men set their Hearts upon
      Turns Ashes — or it prospers; and anon,
        Like Snow upon the Desert's dusty Face
      Lighting a little Hour or two — is gone.

15   And those who husbanded the Golden Grain,
      And those who flung it to the Winds like Rain,
        Alike to no such aureate Earth are turn'd
      As, buried once, Men want dug up again.

16   Think, in this batter'd Caravanserai
Whose Doorways are alternate Night and Day,
    How Sultán after Sultán with his Pomp
Abode his Hour or two, and went his way.

17   They say the Lion and the Lizard keep
The Courts* where Jamshýd gloried and drank deep:
    And Bahrám,* that great Hunter — the Wild Ass
Stamps o'er his Head, and he lies fast asleep.

18   I sometimes think that never blows so red
The Rose as where some buried Cæsar bled;
    That every Hyacinth the Garden wears
Dropt in its Lap from some once lovely Head.

19   And this delightful Herb whose tender Green
Fledges the River's Lip on which we lean —
    Ah, lean upon it lightly! for who knows
From what once Lovely Lip it springs unseen!

B

20 Ah, my Belovéd, fill the cup that clears
    TO-DAY of past Regrets and future Fears —
        To-morrow? — Why, To-morrow I may be
    Myself with Yesterday's Sev'n Thousand Years.*

21 Lo! some we loved, the loveliest and the best
    That Time and Fate of all their Vintage prest,
        Have drunk their Cup a Round or two before,
    And one by one crept silently to Rest.

22 And we, that now make merry in the Room
    They left, and Summer dresses in new Bloom,
        Ourselves must we beneath the Couch of Earth
    Descend, ourselves to make a Couch — for whom?

23 Ah, make the most of what we yet may spend,
    Before we too into the Dust descend;
        Dust into Dust, and under Dust, to lie,
    Sans Wine, sans Song, sans Singer, and — sans End!

24 Alike for those who for TO-DAY prepare,
    And those that after a TO-MORROW stare,
        A Muezzín from the Tower of Darkness cries,
    'Fools! your Reward is neither Here nor There!'

25 Why, all the Saints and Sages who discuss'd
    Of the Two worlds so learnedly, are thrust
        Like foolish Prophets forth; their Words to Scorn
    Are scatter'd, and their Mouths are stopt with Dust.

26 Oh, come with old Khayyám, and leave the Wise
    To talk; one thing is certain, that Life flies;
        One thing is certain, and the Rest is Lies;
    The Flower that once has blown for ever dies.

27 Myself when young did eagerly frequent
    Doctor and Saint, and heard great Argument
        About it and about: but evermore
    Came out by the same Door as in I went.

28   With them the Seed of Wisdom did I sow,
       And with my own hand labour'd it to grow:
          And this was all the Harvest that I reap'd —
       'I came like Water, and like Wind I go.'

29   Into this Universe, and why not knowing,
       Nor whence, like Water willy-nilly flowing!
          And out of it, as Wind along the Waste,
       I know not whither, willy-nilly blowing.

30   What, without asking, hither hurried whence?
       And, without asking, whither hurried hence!
          Another and another Cup to drown
       The Memory of this Impertinence!

31   Up from Earth's Centre through the Seventh Gate
       I rose, and on the Throne of Saturn* sate,
          And many Knots unravel'd by the Road;
       But not the Knot of Human Death and Fate.

32 There was a Door to which I found no Key:
There was a Veil past which I could not see:
   Some little Talk awhile of ME and THEE*
There seem'd — and then no more of THEE and ME.

33 Then to the rolling Heav'n itself I cried,
Asking, 'What Lamp had Destiny to guide
   Her little Children stumbling in the Dark?'
And — 'A blind Understanding!' Heav'n replied.

34 Then to this earthen Bowl did I adjourn
My Lip the secret Well of Life to learn:
   And Lip to Lip it murmur'd — 'While you live
Drink! — for once dead you never shall return.'

35 I think the Vessel, that with fugitive
Articulation answer'd, once did live,
   And merry-make; and the cold Lip I kiss'd
How many Kisses might it take — and give!

36   For in the Market-place, one Dusk of Day,
      I watch'd the Potter thumping his wet Clay:
         And with its all obliterated Tongue
      It murmur'd — 'Gently, Brother, gently, pray!'

37   Ah, fill the Cup: — what boots it to repeat
      How time is slipping underneath our Feet:
         Unborn TO-MORROW and dead YESTERDAY,
      Why fret about them if TO-DAY be sweet!

38   One Moment in Annihilation's Waste,
      One Moment, of the Well of Life to taste —
         The Stars are setting and the Caravan
      Starts for the Dawn of Nothing — Oh, make haste!

39   How long, how long, in infinite Pursuit
      Of This and That endeavour and dispute?
         Better be merry with the fruitful Grape
      Than sadden after none, or bitter, Fruit.

40   You know, my Friends, how long since in my House
     For a new Marriage I did make Carouse:
         Divorced old barren Reason from my Bed,
     And took the Daughter of the Vine to Spouse.

41   For 'IS' and 'IS-NOT' though with Rule and Line,
     And 'UP-AND-DOWN' without, I could define,
         I yet in all I only cared to know,
     Was never deep in anything but — Wine.

42   And lately, by the Tavern Door agape,
     Came stealing through the Dusk an Angel Shape
         Bearing a Vessel on his Shoulder; and
     He bid me taste of it; and 'twas — the Grape!

43   The Grape that can with Logic absolute
     The Two-and-Seventy jarring Sects* confute:
         The subtle Alchemist that in a Trice
     Life's leaden Metal into Gold transmute.

44   The mighty Mahmúd,* the victorious Lord,
      That all the misbelieving and black Horde
         Of Fears and Sorrows that infest the Soul
      Scatters and slays with his enchanted Sword.

45   But leave the wise to wrangle, and with me
      The Quarrel of the Universe let be:
         And, in some corner of the Hubbub coucht,
      Make Game of that which makes as much of Thee.

46   For in and out, above, about, below,
      'Tis nothing but a Magic Shadow-show,
         Play'd in a Box whose Candle is the Sun,
      Round which we Phantom Figures come and go.

47   And if the Wine you drink, the Lip you press,
      End in the Nothing all Things end in — Yes —
         Then fancy while Thou art, Thou art but what
      Thou shalt be — Nothing — Thou shalt not be less.

48　While the Rose blows along the River Brink,
　　With old Khayyám the Ruby Vintage drink:
　　　　And when the Angel with his darker Draught
　　Draws up to Thee — take that, and do not shrink.

49　'Tis all a Chequer-board of Nights and Days
　　Where Destiny with Men for Pieces plays:
　　　　Hither and thither moves, and mates, and slays,
　　And one by one back in the Closet lays.

50　The Ball no Question makes of Ayes and Noes,
　　But Right or Left as strikes the Player goes;
　　　　And He that toss'd Thee down into the Field,
　　He knows about it all — He knows — HE knows!

51　The Moving Finger writes; and, having writ,
　　Moves on: nor all thy Piety nor Wit
　　　　Shall lure it back to cancel half a Line,
　　Nor all thy Tears wash out a Word of it.

52   And that inverted Bowl we call The Sky,
      Whereunder crawling coop't we live and die,
          Lift not thy hands to It for help — for It
      Rolls impotently on as Thou or I.

53   With Earth's first Clay They did the Last Man's knead,
      And then of the Last Harvest sow'd the Seed:
          Yea, the first Morning of Creation wrote
      What the Last Dawn of Reckoning shall read.

54   I Tell Thee this — When, starting from the Goal,
      Over the shoulders of the flaming Foal
          Of Heav'n Parwín and Mushtara* they flung,
      In my predestin'd Plot of Dust and Soul.

55   The Vine had struck a Fibre; which about
      If clings my Being — let the Súfi* flout;
          Of my Base Metal may be filed a Key,
      That shall unlock the Door he howls without.

56 And this I know: whether the one True Light
   Kindle to Love, or Wrath consume me quite,
      One glimpse of It within the Tavern caught
   Better than in the Temple lost outright.

57 Oh Thou, who didst with Pitfall and with Gin
   Beset the Road I was to wander in,
      Thou wilt not with Predestination round
   Enmesh me, and impute my Fall to Sin?

58 Oh Thou, who Man of baser Earth didst make,
   And who with Eden didst devise the Snake;
      For all the Sin wherewith the Face of man
   Is blacken'd, Man's Forgiveness give — and take!

KUZA NÁMA

59 Listen again. One evening at the Close
   Of Ramazán,* ere the better Moon arose,
      In that old Potter's Shop I stood alone
   With the clay Population round in Rows.

60   And, strange to tell, among that Earthen Lot
        Some could articulate, while others not:
            And suddenly one more impatient cried —
        'Who is the Potter, pray, and who the Pot?'

61   Then said another — 'Surely not in vain
        My Substance from the common Earth was ta'en;
            That He who subtly wrought me into Shape
        Should stamp me back to common Earth again.'

62   Another said — 'Why, ne'er a peevish Boy
        Would break the Bowl from which he drank in Joy;
            Shall He that made the Vessel in pure Love
        And Fancy, in an after Rage destroy!'

63   None answer'd this; but after Silence spake
        A Vessel of a more ungainly Make:
            'They sneer at me for leaning all awry;
        What! did the Hand then of the Potter shake?'

64   Said one — 'Folks of a surly Tapster tell,
      And daub his Visage with the Smoke of Hell;
          They talk of some strict Testing of us — Pish!
      He's a Good Fellow and 'twill all be well.'

65   Then said another with a long-drawn Sigh,
      'My Clay with long Oblivion is gone dry:
          But, fill me with the old familiar Juice,
      Methinks I might recover by-and-bye!'

66   So while the Vessels one by one were speaking,
      One spied the little Crescent all were seeking:
          And then they jogged each other, 'Brother! Brother!
      Hark to the Porter's Shoulder-knot a-creaking!'

67   Ah, with the Grape my fading Life provide,
      And wash my Body whence the Life has died,
          And in a Windingsheet of Vine-leaf wrapt,
      So bury me by some sweet Garden-side.

68 That ev'n my buried Ashes such a Snare
    Of Perfume shall fling up into the Air,
        As not a True Believer passing by
    But shall be overtaken unaware.

69 Indeed the Idols I have loved so long
    Have done my Credit in Men's Eye much wrong:
        Have drown'd my Honour in a shallow Cup,
    And sold my Reputation for a Song.

70 Indeed, indeed, Repentance oft before
    I swore — but was I sober when I swore?
        And then and then came Spring, and Rose-in-hand
    My thread-bare Penitence a-pieces tore.

71 And much as Wine has play'd the Infidel,
    And robb'd me of my Robe of Honour — well,
        I often wonder what the Vintners buy
    One half so precious as the Goods they sell.

72 Alas, that Spring should vanish with the Rose!
    That Youth's sweet-scented Manuscript should close!
        The Nightingale that in the Branches sang,
    Ah, whence, and whither flown again, who knows!

73 Ah, Love! could thou and I with Fate conspire
    To grasp this sorry Scheme of Things entire,
        Would not we shatter it to bits — and then
    Re-mould it nearer to the Heart's Desire!

74 Ah, Moon of my Delight who know'st no wane,
    The Moon of Heaven is rising once again:
        How oft hereafter rising shall she look
    Through this same Garden after me — in vain!

75 And when Thyself with shining Foot shall pass
    Among the Guests Star-scatter'd on the Grass
        And in thy joyous Errand reach the Spot
    Where I made one — turn down an empty Glass!

TAMÁM SHUD

NOTES